I0762486
MADONNA
WHOHQ

This is dedicated to my sister, who actually called the cable company and said, "I want my MTV." I would not be the man I am today if she hadn't done that—FS

To my mom, Olga, for giving me my first Madonna CD on my birthday in the '90s, *The Immaculate Collection*—CM

PENGUIN WORKSHOP
An imprint of Penguin Random House LLC
1745 Broadway, New York, NY 10019
penguinrandomhouse.com

Design by Taylor Abatiell
Text set in Adobe Garamond Pro

The art was created using Wacom Cintiq 16" and Photoshop 2020.

Library of Congress Cataloging-in-Publication Data is available.

First published in the United States of America by Penguin Workshop, 2026

Manufactured in China
HH

ISBN 9798217053551
10 9 8 7 6 5 4 3 2 1

The authorized representative in the EU for product safety and compliance is Penguin Random House Ireland, Morrison Chambers, 32 Nassau Street, Dublin D02 YH68, Ireland, https://eu-contact.penguin.ie.

MADONNA

A WHO HQ ILLUSTRATED BIOGRAPHY

by
Francesco Sedita

illustrated by
Claudia Marianno

PENGUIN WORKSHOP

On October 14, 2023, a crowd of nearly twenty thousand people stood in excitement at London's O2 Arena. A thump echoed through the space, and the lights went down.

A collective gasp swept through the stadium. A glamorous figure draped in black rose from center stage and began singing, "When I was very young, nothing really mattered to me but making myself happy. I was the only one. Now that I am grown, everything's changed. I'll never be the same . . . because of you!"

She opened her arms in a loving embrace to her adoring fans.

Who was this iconic pop star?

On August 16, 1958, Madonna Louise Veronica Ciccone was born into a big family in Bay City, Michigan. She was named after her mother, and her parents had six children.

When Madonna was just five years old, her mother passed away due to cancer. Her father, Silvio, married again, and Madonna had more siblings—it must have been hard to stand out in such a big family!

This moment in her young life would inform much of the art she created when she grew up. She became a motherly figure to her fans, her dancers, and her friends. And later, she became a mother to six children of her own.

According to friends, she was a sensitive and shy girl. Madonna took tap lessons and preteen jazz. When she got older, she was a cheerleader. But living in her small town and performing in shows at West Middle School would not be enough to keep her mind—and her spirit—fulfilled.

She attended the University of Michigan in Ann Arbor in 1976. She'd been awarded a four-year scholarship to their dance program. But in 1977, she applied for and received a scholarship to New York City's Alvin Ailey American Dance Theater.

Madonna left Michigan and moved to the East Village section of New York City. She had only thirty-five dollars in her pocket.

Soon, she fell into New York City's legendary club scene and went dancing at places like Danceteria, an enormous nightclub known in the 1980s for its powerful sound system.

It was there that she convinced Mark Kamins, a DJ who picked the music for the dance floor, to play a song she wrote and recorded called "Everybody." When he saw the crowd loving it, he decided to help Madonna find a record label to make her music. She signed with Sire Records and began working on her first album.

In 1984, when she was just about to release her second studio album, *Like a Virgin*, MTV asked Madonna to perform on their first Video Music Awards show. Being asked to do this was a big honor and step forward in her career.

She wanted to do something to surprise the audience and considered bringing a white Bengal tiger onstage. Instead, she appeared standing atop a seventeen-foot-tall wedding cake. She slowly marched down the side of the cake, pulled off her veil, and threw her bouquet at the audience. She finished the song as she rolled on the floor, the cameras struggling to keep up with her.

Mission accomplished! The audience was stunned! Some people wondered if she'd ruined her career by acting so outrageously and not just doing what was expected.

I WANT MY MTV!

On August 1, 1981, a brand-new television channel debuted to the surprise of parents and the delight of teenagers: MTV. MTV, or Music Television, was a network devoted to showing music videos from all the newest and hottest performers, from rock bands like the Rolling Stones, Dire Straits, and Men at Work to pop singers like Madonna, the Go-Go's, Duran Duran, and Janet Jackson. Later, stars like Britney Spears, the Backstreet Boys, and Christina Aguilera made legendary videos, too. This form of art—short films set to music—was new to the world. It was an exciting way to show the hottest stars dancing and performing.

The first video ever played on the channel was for a song called "Video Killed the Radio Star" by the Buggles.

"Video Killed the Radio Star" by the Buggles

"Smells Like Teen Spirit" by Nirvana

"Scream" by Michael Jackson and Janet Jackson

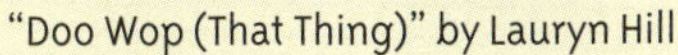

"Doo Wop (That Thing)" by Lauryn Hill

"Ironic" by Alanis Morissette

"Toxic" by Britney Spears

In 1989, after enjoying more hits like "Lucky Star," "Material Girl," and "Live to Tell," Madonna made a bold statement with her new album *Like a Prayer*. The music was still dancey and poppy, but now a new Madonna emerged: Not only was she no longer blond, but she was also writing music that would challenge institutions like the government and the church. Her songs focused on family, love, and the loss of her mother. She was no longer just the "Material Girl" or a misbehaved bride, **she was a rebel who challenged the world around her with her music and performances.**

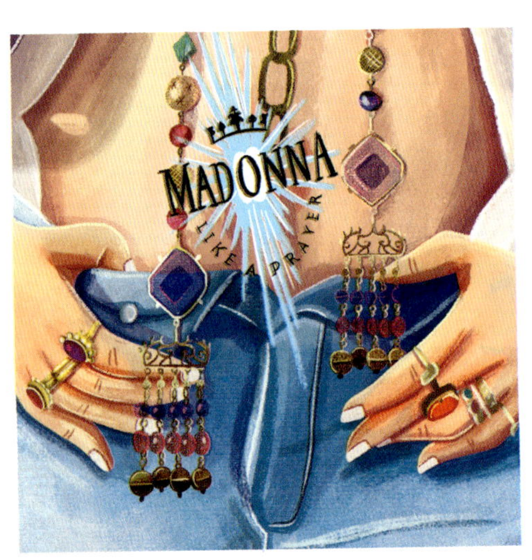

Soon after, she delivered a one-two-three punch to her fans. She announced a new movie role as Breathless Mahoney in *Dick Tracy*, a fifty-seven-stop world tour called Blond Ambition, and a black-and-white documentary movie of her tour, called *Madonna: Truth or Dare*.

Madonna had a film crew follow her and the dancers, singers, and backstage team throughout the tour, recording every moment of their hard work and fun.

MADONNA AT THE MOVIES

Desperately Seeking Susan

Throughout her career, Madonna acted in many movies. Before *Dick Tracy* and *Madonna: Truth or Dare*, she appeared in her first big film role as the title character in *Desperately Seeking Susan*, where she played a character similar to herself who resided in the East Village in the film. That was in 1985.

Shortly after, she played Nikki Flynn, a fun and wacky character with a pet leopard, in *Who's That Girl?*

As well as starring in *Dick Tracy*, she sang "Sooner or Later (I Always Get My Man)," a new song for the film written just for her by the

Who's That Girl?

famous composer Stephen Sondheim. She performed the song at the Academy Awards in March 1991, where it won the award for Best Music, Original Song.

Academy Awards performance

Then in 1996, she played the main character in *Evita*. This was a movie version of the famous musical by Andrew Lloyd Webber and Tim Rice based on the life of Argentinian political figure Eva Perón. People thought she got the part because she was famous, not because she was the best actress for it. But her performance won a Golden Globe for Best Actress in a Motion Picture, Comedy or Musical. The movie also won three other Golden Globes, including Best Motion Picture, Comedy or Musical.

Evita

During this time, Madonna released a new song called "Vogue," and it topped *Billboard*'s Hot 100 chart for three consecutive weeks. It remains one of her most celebrated hits.

The song—and video—introduced many of her listeners to a dance style called voguing, made popular in underground dance ballrooms in New York City.

The style appears simple: Dancers make modeling poses to the beat of the music. But the people in ballroom communities created voguing competitions and even awarded trophies to the best dancers!

Madonna was already known for bringing different sounds and musical inspirations to her music, and with the song "Vogue," she proved she not only had her ear to the ground but her foot in the door of the coolest new ideas.

After so much time in the spotlight and the release of two more studio albums, Madonna took a step back after the birth of her first child, Lourdes, or Lola as she calls her. “When my daughter was born,” Madonna told TV host Oprah Winfrey, “I was born again.” Almost four years later, she had her first son, Rocco.

When she returned with her seventh studio album, *Ray of Light*, she introduced the world to a very different, softer side of herself: Madonna as Earth Mother. She also practiced Kabbalah now, which is a type of Jewish mysticism that talks about ways to understand God and the universe.

The album won the Grammy Award in 1999 for Best Pop Album.

Over the years, as she continued to make her music, Madonna became very passionate about the well-being of those in Africa, especially the many children who needed assistance and care in Malawi. In 2006, she helped to create an organization called Raising Malawi. It was through this work that Madonna met and adopted four children: David Banda, Mercy James, and twins Estere and Stella.

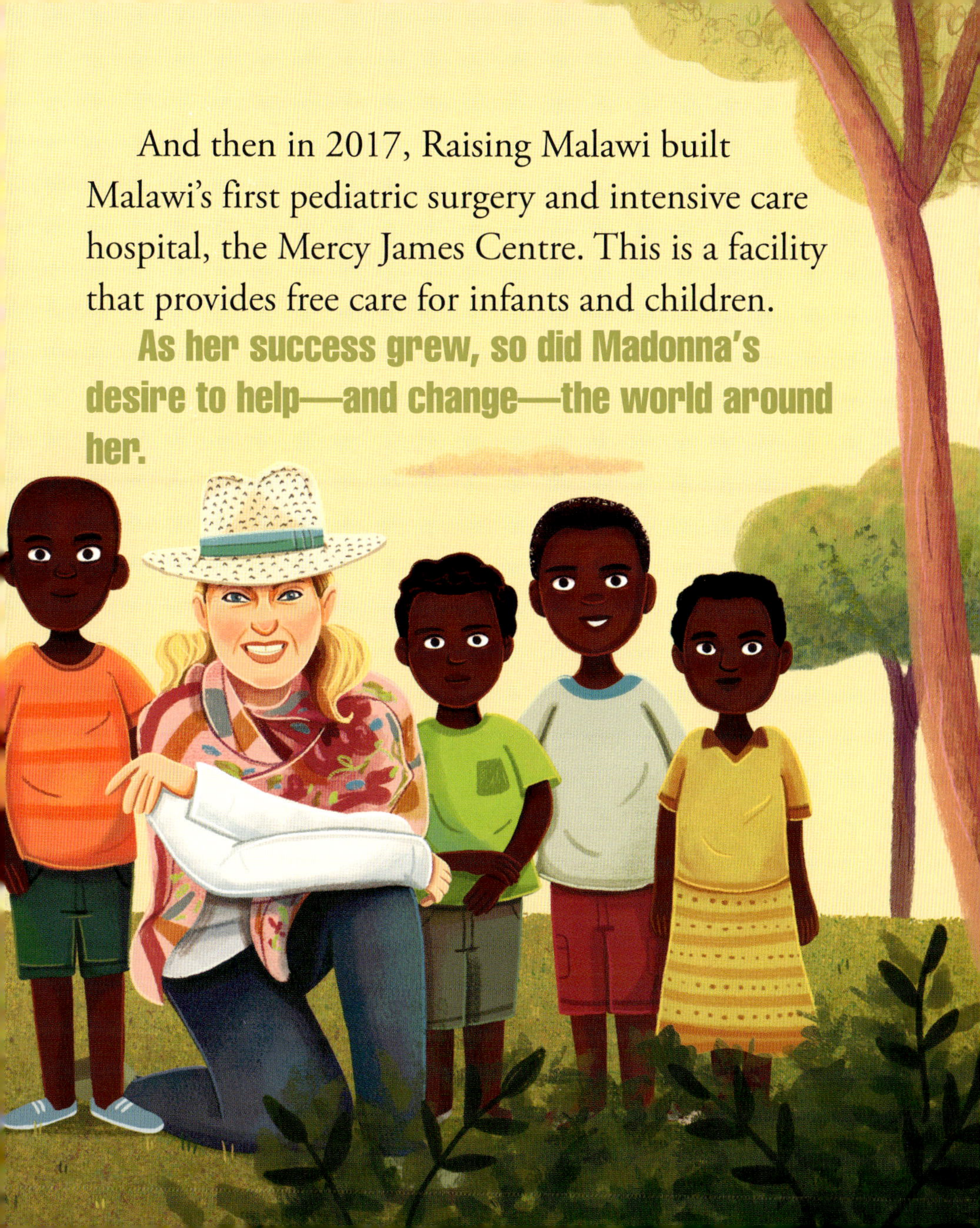

And then in 2017, Raising Malawi built Malawi's first pediatric surgery and intensive care hospital, the Mercy James Centre. This is a facility that provides free care for infants and children.

As her success grew, so did Madonna's desire to help—and change—the world around her.

Throughout her career, Madonna has proven herself to be a dedicated activist, urging her listeners to affect change and to speak up against prejudice and oppression. On albums like *American Life*, *Rebel Heart*, and *Madame X*, she sings songs of revolution.

As she's become more and more famous, one thing has been very clear: Madonna does not take no for an answer, and she protects her fans and their rights, including by singing songs of their freedom. Over her many years in the spotlight, she has become a partner to those who need her help and her voice. She has passionately spoken up for LGBTQ+ rights, marched for Black Lives Matter, and used her social media to address injustices she sees in the world around her.

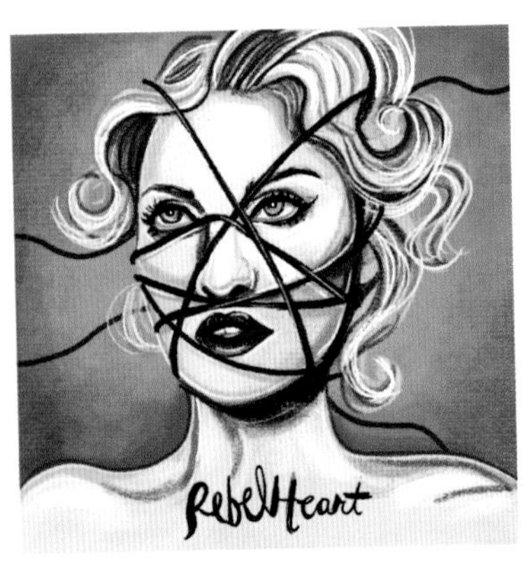

WE STAND WITH YOU
BLACK LIVES MATTER
BLACK
BLACK BLACK BLACK

On December 9, 2016, Madonna was named *Billboard*'s Woman of the Year. This award celebrates women who have made great and lasting contributions to the music industry, while inspiring other women to pursue careers in music. Other artists to receive this award include Reba McEntire, Beyoncé, Taylor Swift (twice!), and SZA.

Madonna delivered an emotional acceptance speech. She talked about her time in New York City, the friends she lost to the AIDS epidemic, and the people who supported her throughout her career.

"People say I'm so controversial," she said in her speech. "But I think the most controversial thing I have ever done is to stick around."

She concluded by saying, "As women, we have to start appreciating our own worth and each other's worth. Seek out strong women to befriend, to align yourself with, to learn from, to be inspired by, to collaborate with, to support, to be enlightened by."

On May 4, 2024, after seventy-nine performances around the globe, Madonna's Celebration Tour took to the stage one final time. But this wasn't just any concert. Madonna decided to end the tour with a free show on Copacabana Beach in Rio de Janeiro, Brazil. An estimated 1.6 million people attended!

All at once a pop icon, record breaker, rebel, mother, and epically talented artist, Madonna floated up from beneath the stage. Her fans from all over the world stood, breathless.

". . . I'll never be the same . . . because of you!"

BIBLIOGRAPHY

Billboard Staff. "Madonna Is Billboard's 2016 Woman of the Year." ***Billboard***, October 14, 2016. https://www.billboard.com/music/awards/madonna-2016-woman-of-the-year-7541832/.

Croft, Malcolm. ***The Little Guide to Madonna: Express Yourself***. London: Orange Hippo!, 2023.

Gabriel, Mary. ***Madonna: A Rebel Life***. New York: Little, Brown and Company, 2023.

WEBSITE

www.raisingmalawi.org

TIMELINE

1958 — Madonna Louise Veronica Ciccone is born August 16 in Bay City, Michigan

1978 — Leaves her hometown and moves to the East Village section of New York City

1985 — *Desperately Seeking Susan* premieres

1990 — Becomes the first woman entrepreneur to appear on a *Forbes* magazine cover

Eighth album, *Music*, is released and debuts at number one on the *Billboard* 200 chart — 2000

Performs at the Super Bowl halftime show — 2012

Named Goodwill Ambassador for Child Welfare by President Mutharika of Malawi — 2014

Concludes the Celebration Tour in Rio de Janeiro, with a free concert on Copacabana Beach; an estimated 1.6 million people attend — 2024

WHOHQ
MADONNA